THE MOST REQUESTED
Country Songs

ISBN 978-1-4803-9095-9

cherry lane
music company

EXCLUSIVELY DISTRIBUTED BY

HAL•LEONARD®
CORPORATION
7777 W. BLUEMOUND RD. P.O. BOX 13819 MILWAUKEE, WI 53213

Visit Hal Leonard Online at
www.halleonard.com

CONTENTS

AIN'T NOTHING 'BOUT YOU

Words and Music by TOM SHAPIRO
and RIVERS RUTHERFORD

Once I thought that love was some-thin' I could nev-er do. ___
In my life I've been ___ ham-mered by some heav-y blows ___

Nev-er knew that I could feel this much. But this yearn-in' in the
that ___ nev-er knocked me off my feet. All you got-ta do is

BEAUTIFUL MESS

Words and Music by SONNY LeMAIRE,
CLAY MILLS and SHANE MINOR

A BETTER MAN

Words and Music by JAMES HAYDEN NICHOLAS
and CLINT BLACK

BRING ON THE RAIN

Words and Music by BILLY MONTANA
and HELEN DARLING

I'd like to hide a-way some-where and lock the door. A

sin - gle bat - tle lost, but not the war. 'Cause to - mor - row's an -

oth - er day and I'm thirst - y an - y - way, so bring on the

rain. It's

24

not gon-na let it get _____ me down. _____

I'm not gon-na cry. _____

So bring on the rain. _____

Ooh. _____

CAN'T FIGHT THE MOONLIGHT

Words and Music by
DIANE WARREN

Moderately slow

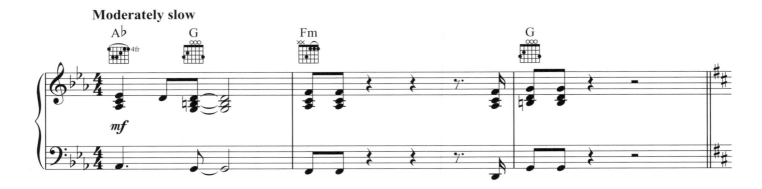

Un-der a lov-er's sky, gon-na be with you, and no
There's no es-cape from love once the gen-tle breeze weaves

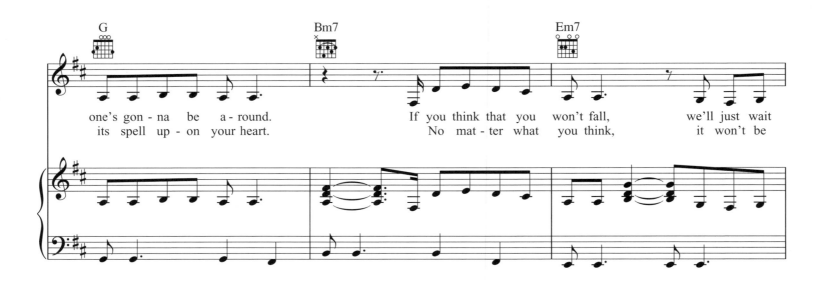

one's gon-na be a-round. If you think that you won't fall, we'll just wait
its spell up-on your heart. No mat-ter what you think, it won't be

CHICKEN FRIED

Words and Music by ZAC BROWN
and WYATT DURRETTE

*Recorded a half step lower.

CONCRETE ANGEL

Words and Music by STEPHANIE BENTLEY
and ROB CROSBY

COUNTRY GIRL
(Shake It for Me)

Words and Music by LUKE BRYAN
and DALLAS DAVIDSON

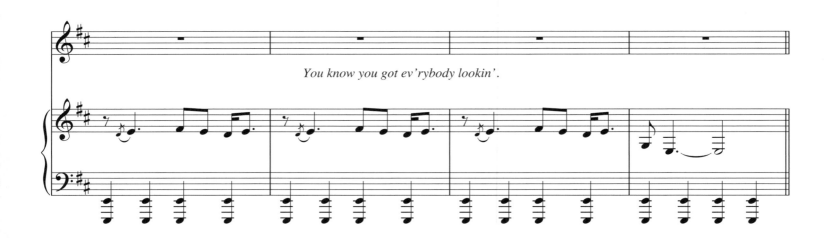

Coun-try girl, shake it for me, girl, shake it for me,

girl, shake it for me.

Guitar solo

Solo ends   Now

dance   like a dan - de - lion __ in the wind, on the hill un - der - neath the pines. __ Yeah,

move   like the riv - er flows, __ feel __ the kick drum down deep in your toes. __

53

Coun-try girl, shake it for me, ___ girl, ___ shake it for me, ___ girl, ___ shake it for me.

CRUISE

Words and Music by CHASE RICE,
TYLER HUBBARD, BRIAN KELLEY,
JOEY MOI and JESSE RICE

Ba - by, you a song. You make me wan - na roll ___ my win - dows down and

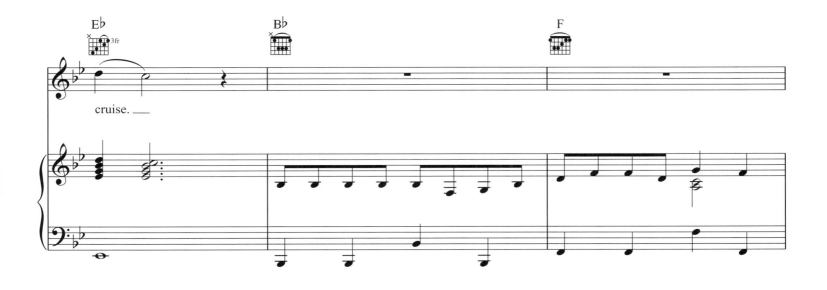

cruise. ___

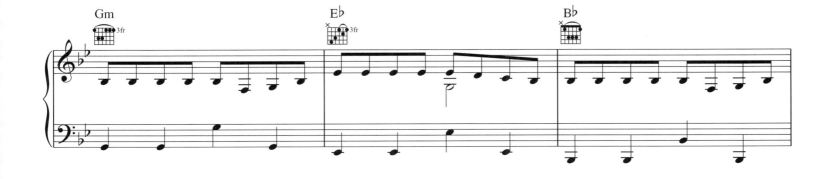

DON'T TAKE THE GIRL

Words and Music by LARRY JOHNSON
and CRAIG MARTIN

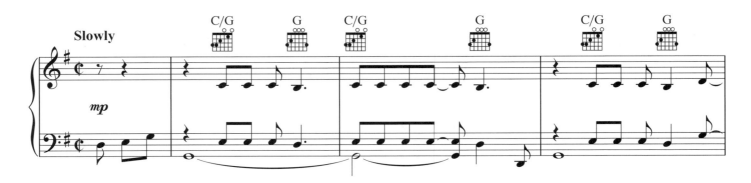

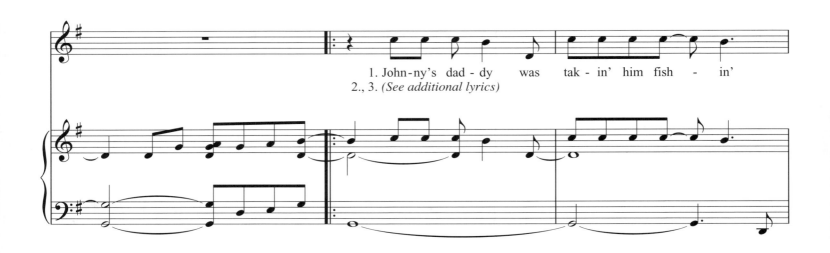

1. John-ny's dad-dy was tak-in' him fish-in'
2., 3. *(See additional lyrics)*

when he was eight years old. ___ A lit-tle girl ___ came through ___

Johnny's daddy was takin' him fishin' when he was eight years old.

Additional Lyrics

2. Same ol' boy, same sweet girl, ten years down the road.
   He held her tight and kissed her lips in front of the picture show.
   A stranger came and pulled a gun and grabbed her by the arm.
   Said, "If you do what I tell you to, there won't be any harm."
   And Johnny said,
   "Take my money, take my wallet, take my credit cards.
   Here's the watch that my grandpa gave me, here's the key to my car.
   Mister, give it a whirl, but please, don't take the girl."

3. Same ol' boy, same sweet girl, five years down the road.
   There's gonna be a little one and she says, "It's time to go."
   Doctor says, "The baby's fine, but you'll have to leave
   'Cause his mama's fadin' fast," and Johnny hit his knees.
   And then he prayed,
   "Take the very breath you gave me, take the heart from my chest.
   I'll gladly take her place if you'll let me. Make this my last request:
   Take me out of this world. God, please, don't take the girl."

DON'T YOU WANNA STAY

Words and Music by JASON SELLERS,
PAUL JENKINS and ANDREW GIBSON

Moderately fast

Male: I real - ly hate to let _____ this mo - ment go, _____
Female: Let's take it slow, I don't _____ wan - na move too

_____ fast.
I don't wan - na just make love, _____
touch - in' your skin and your _____

* Recorded a half step higher.

DOWNTOWN

Words and Music by NATALIE HEMBY,
LUKE LAIRD and SHANE McANALLY

__ all the par-ties on the streets are talk-in', store-front man-ne-quins sleep-in' in lights.

EVERY TIME I HEAR YOUR NAME

Words and Music by KEITH ANDERSON,
JEFFREY STEELE and TOM HAMBRIDGE

* *Recorded a half step lower.*

rain fall - in' right out of the blue ___ sky. And it's the fifth of May ___
caught in the "you were the on - ly one ___ for me" kind - a thought, _

___ and I'm right there star - in' in your ___ eyes. And noth - in's
___ and your face is all ___ that I ___ see. I know I can't go

changed, you're still the same. ___ And I ___ get
back, but I still go back. ___ And there _ we

lost in the in - no - cence of a first ___ kiss. And I'm hang - in' on ___
are, parked _ down by the riv - er - side and I'm in your arms, _

FLY OVER STATES

Words and Music by NEIL THRASHER
and MICHAEL DULANEY

been through In - di - an - a,

on the plains _ of O - kla - ho - ma?

Take a ride. _____

FOLLOW YOUR ARROW

Words and Music by KACEY MUSGRAVES,
SHANE McANALLY and BRANDY CLARK

Moderately

If you save your-self for mar-riage, you're a bore. __ If you don't save your-self for mar-riage, you're a hor-ri-ble per-son. __ If you won't have a drink, __ then you're a prude. __ But they'll call you a drunk __ as soon as you down __ the first one. __ If

GOOD MORNING BEAUTIFUL

Words and Music by TODD CERNEY
and ZACK LYLE

Good morn - ing, ___ beau - ti - ful,

how was your ___ night? _____ Mine was won - der - ful ___ with

you by my side. ___ And when I o - pened my ___ eyes ___ to

HOW DO YOU LIKE ME NOW?!

Words and Music by TOBY KEITH
and CHUCK CANNON

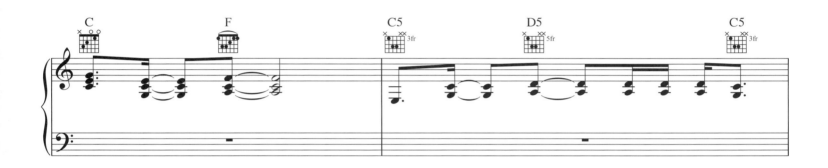

Yeah,

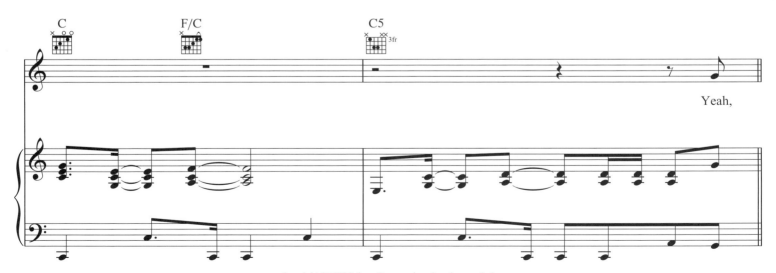

Solo ends How do you like ___ me now, ___ now that I'm on ___ my

way? Do you still think ___ I'm cra - zy stand - in' here ___ to - day? ___

___ I could - n't make ___ you love ___ me, but I al - ways dreamed a -

bout liv - in' in ___ your ra - di - o. ___ How do you like ___ me now? ___

Repeat and Fade

Optional Ending

THE GOOD STUFF

Words and Music by CRAIG WISEMAN
and JIM COLLINS

GUNPOWDER & LEAD

Words and Music by MIRANDA LAMBERT
and HEATHER LITTLE

Coun - ty Road   Two - thir - ty - three

un - der my feet,

gun - pow - der and lead. ___

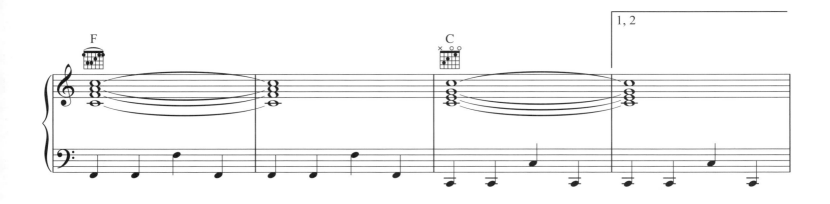

Guitar solo ad lib.

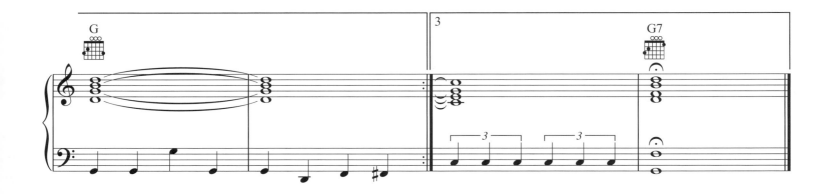

I KNEW YOU WERE TROUBLE.

Words and Music by TAYLOR SWIFT,
SHELLBACK and MAX MARTIN

Moderately fast

Once up-on a time a
No a-pol-o-gies, he'll

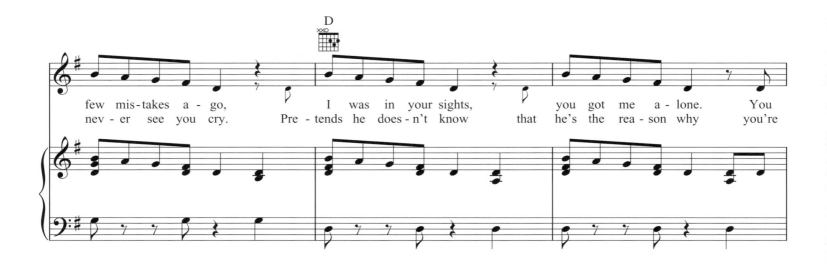

few mis-takes a-go, I was in your sights, you got me a-lone. You
nev-er see you cry. Pre-tends he does-n't know that he's the rea-son why you're

found _____ me, you found _____ me, you found _____ me, ee,
drown _____ ing, you're drown _____ ing, you're drown _____ ing, ing,

I STILL BELIEVE IN YOU

Words and Music by JOHN BARLOW JARVIS
and VINCE GILL

1. Ev-'ry-bod-y wants a lit-tle piece of my time, but still I put you at the
2. (See additional lyrics)

end of the line. How it breaks my heart to cause you this pain,

to see the tears you cry fall-in' like rain. Give me the chance

ba - by, I still __ be - lieve in __ you. Ba - by,

you __ and me.

rit.

Additional Lyrics

2. Somewhere along the way, I guess I just lost track,
   Only thinkin' of myself, never lookin' back.
   For all the times I've hurt you, I apologize,
   I'm sorry it took so long to finally realize.
   Give me the chance to prove
   That nothing's worth losing you.
   Chorus

I SWEAR

Words and Music by FRANK MYERS
and GARY BAKER

I see the ques - tions in ___ your eyes; ___ I know what's weigh -
I'll give you ev - 'ry - thing ___ I can; ___ I'll build your dreams _

IF I DIE YOUNG

Words and Music by
KIMBERLY PERRY

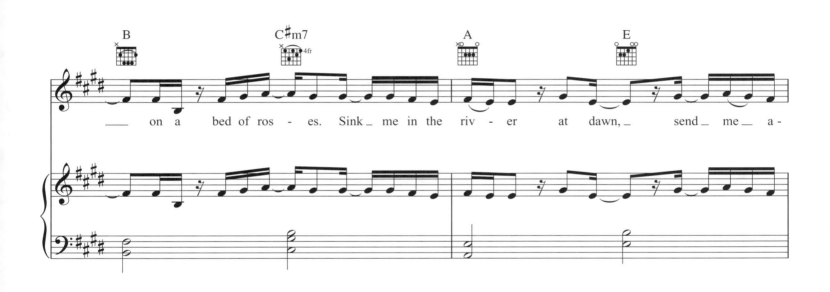

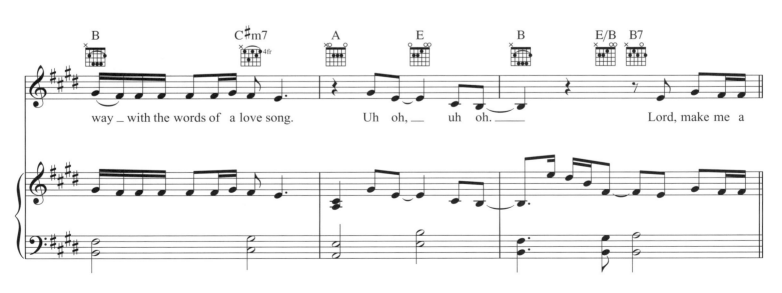

So put on your best, _ boys, and I'll wear my pearls. What I nev-er did is done. A pen-ny for my thoughts: oh no, _ I'll sell _ 'em for a dol-lar. They're worth so much more af - ter I'm a gon-er. And _ may-be then you'll hear the words _ I've been sing-ing. Fun-ny, when you're dead how peo-

IF YOU'RE GOING THROUGH HELL
(Before the Devil Even Knows)

Words and Music by ANNIE TATE,
SAM TATE and DAVE BERG

Well, you know __ __ those times when you feel like there's a sign __ there on your back, says, "I
deep down in that __ dark-ness, I've been down __ to my last match. Felt a

If you're

dev - il e - ven knows you're there. _____

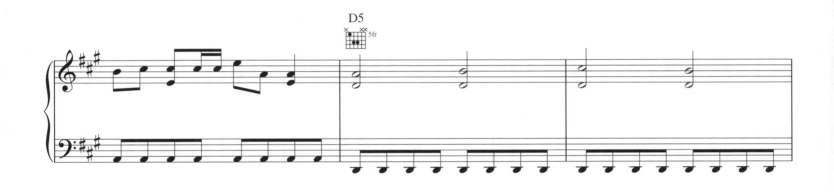

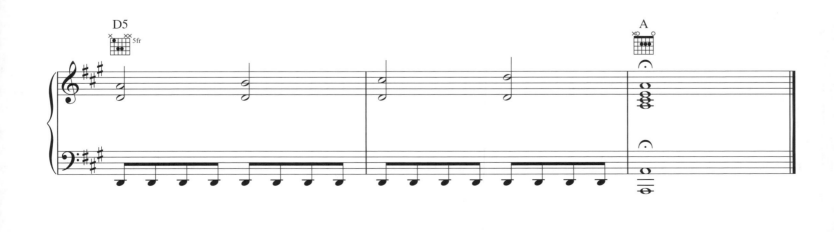

LITTLE BIT OF EVERYTHING

Words and Music by BRAD WARREN,
BRETT WARREN and KEVIN RUDOLPH

Moderately fast

I wish I _____ could take a cab down _____

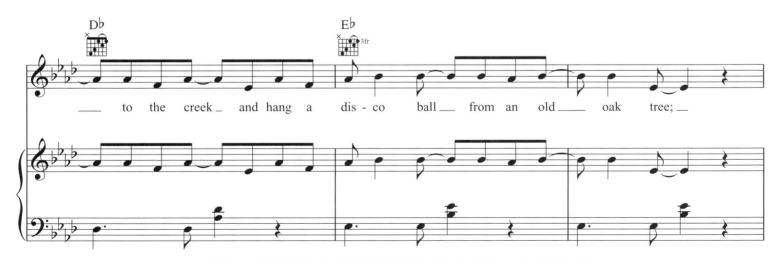

_____ to the creek _____ and hang a dis - co ball _____ from an old _____ oak tree; _____

IT'S A GREAT DAY TO BE ALIVE

Words and Music by
DARRELL SCOTT

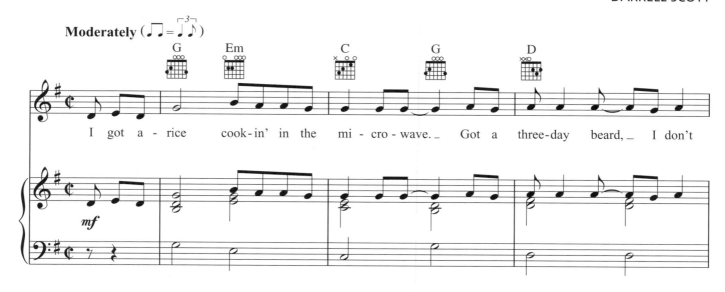

I got a - rice cook - in' in the mi - cro - wave. __ Got a three - day beard, __ I don't

plan to shave. __ And it's a goof - y thing, but I just got - ta say, __ hey,

I'm a - do - in' al - right. Yeah, I think I'll make me some home - made soup.

just this good? _____

It's been fif - teen years ___ since I ___ left home ___ and
look in the mir - ror and what do I see? A

said good luck ___ to ev - 'ry seed I'd sown. ___ Gave it my best and then I
lone wolf there ___ star - in' back at me. ___ Long in the tooth, ___ but harm -

left it a - lone. _____ I hope they're do - in' al - right. Now, I
- less as can be. _____ Lord, I guess he's do - in' al -

Ow - ooh _____

LITTLE WHITE CHURCH

Words and Music by JIMI WESTBROOK,
KIMBERLY SCHLAPMAN, KAREN FAIRCHILD,
PHILLIP SWEET and WAYNE KIRKPATRICK

You've been sing - in' that same old song
ride _____ this gra - vy train _____
dev - il, sil - ver tongue, _____

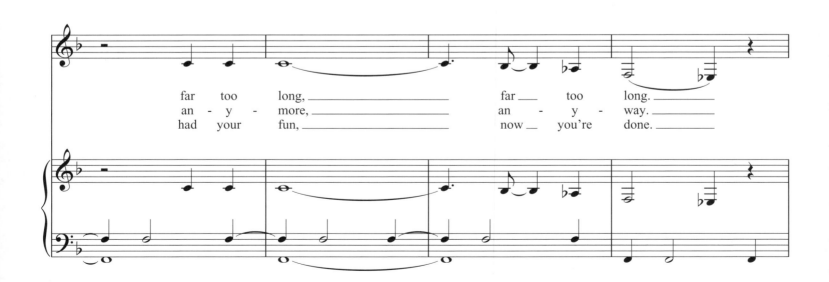

far too long, _____ far _____ too long. _____
an - y - more, _____ an - y - way. _____
had your fun, _____ now _____ you're done. _____

You can't Take me down,

come on. *Instrumental*

Instrumental ends

MUD ON THE TIRES

Words and Music by BRAD PAISLEY
and CHRIS DUBOIS

I've got some big news. The bank fin-'lly came through and I'm hold-in' the keys to a brand-new Chev-ro-let.

Moon-light on a duck blind, cat-fish on a trot line. ___

Sun sets a-bout ___ nine this time of year. ___

We can throw a blan-ket down, crick-ets sing-in' in the back-ground ___

MUST BE DOIN' SOMETHIN' RIGHT

Words and Music by PATRICK MATTHEWS
and MARTY DODSON

REDNECK WOMAN

Words and Music by GRETCHEN WILSON
and JOHN RICH

Well, I ain't nev - er
Se - cret,

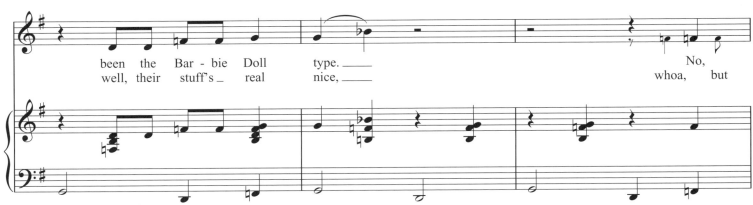

been the Bar - bie Doll type. _____
well, their stuff's _ real nice, _____

No,
whoa, but

Recorded a half step lower.

here's to all ___ my sis - ters out there keep-in' it ___ coun - try. ___

___ Let me get a big ___ "Hell, yeah" ___ from the

red - neck girls like me. Hell, yeah. ___ (Hell,

yeah!) Vic - to - ri - a's

NEED YOU NOW

Words and Music by HILLARY SCOTT,
CHARLES KELLEY, DAVE HAYWOOD
and JOSH KEAR

19 SOMETHIN'

Words and Music by CHRIS DUBOIS
and DAVID LEE

RED SOLO CUP

Words and Music by JIM BEAVERS,
BRETT WARREN, BRETT BEAVERS
and BRAD WARREN

Now a Red Solo Cup is the best receptacle for barbecues, tailgates, fairs and festivals.
Now I really love how you're easy to stack. But I really hate how you're easy to crack.
Now I've seen you in blue and I've seen you in yellow. But only you, red, will do for this fellow,

And you, sir, do not have a pair of testicles if you prefer drinkin' from glass.
'Cause when beer runs down in front of my back, well, that my friends, is quite yucky.
'cause you're the Abbott unto my Costello and you are the fruit to my loom.

A Red Solo Cup is cheap and disposable. In fourteen years they are decomposable.
But I have to admit that the ladies get smitten, admirin' how sharply my first name is written
Red Solo Cup, you're more than just plastic, you're more than amazing, you're more than fantastic.

SEE YOU AGAIN

Words and Music by HILLARY LINDSEY,
DAVID HODGES and CARRIE UNDERWOOD

Moderately

SPRINGSTEEN

Words and Music by ERIC CHURCH,
JEFFERY HYDE and RYAN TYNDELL

To this day__ when I hear that song,__ I see you stand - in' there on that lawn,__ dis-count shades,__ store-bought tan,__ flip flops and cut - off jeans.__ Some-where be-tween that set - tin' sun,__

STORM WARNING

Words and Music by busbee,
GORDIE SAMPSON and HUNTER HAYES

Moderately fast

warn - in'.

A lit - tle heads up, lit - tle more time, a lit - tle lee - way, some kind of sign

STUCK LIKE GLUE

Words and Music by SHY CARTER,
KRISTIAN BUSH, JENNIFER NETTLES
and KEVIN GRIFFIN

Lyrics:

Ab-so-lute-ly no one that knows me ___ bet-ter,

no ___ one that can make me feel so ___ good.

How ___ did we stay so long to-geth-er when ev-

* Recorded a half step lower.

THAT DON'T IMPRESS ME MUCH

Words and Music by SHANIA TWAIN
and R.J. LANGE

Moderately

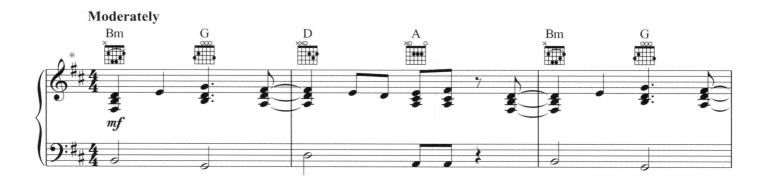

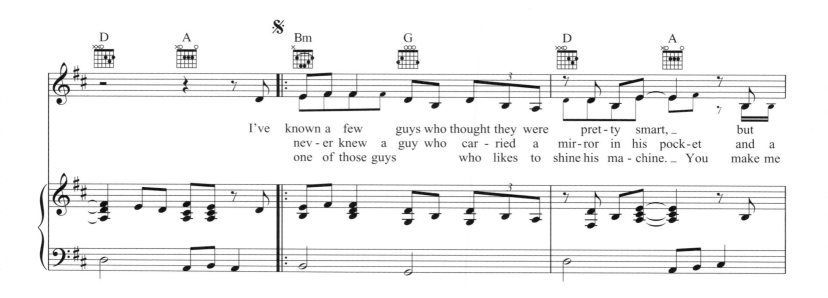

I've known a few guys who thought they were pret-ty smart, _ but
nev-er knew a guy who car-ried a mir-ror in his pock-et and a
one of those guys who likes to shine his ma-chine. _ You make me

you've got be-ing right down _ to an art. _ You think you're a gen-ius, you drive me
comb _ up his sleeve just in case. And all that ex-tra-hold gel in your
take off my shoes be-fore you let me get in. I can't be-lieve you kiss your

* Recorded a half step lower.

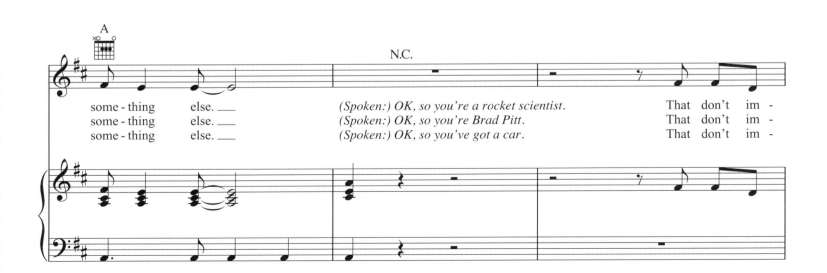

(Spoken:) OK, so what do you

think, you're Elvis or something?   Whatever.

That don't im - press __ me.

THIS KISS

Words and Music by ANNIE ROBOFF,
BETH NIELSEN CHAPMAN and ROBIN LERNER

I don't want an-oth-er heart-break. I don't need an-oth-er turn to cry, _____ no.
Cin-der - el - la said to Snow White, "How does love get so off course?" _____ Oh.

I don't want to learn the hard way. Ba - by, hel - lo, oh no, good - bye.
All I want-ed was a white knight with a good heart, soft touch, fast horse.

It's, ah, ___ sub - lim - i - nal. This kiss, ___ this kiss. ___

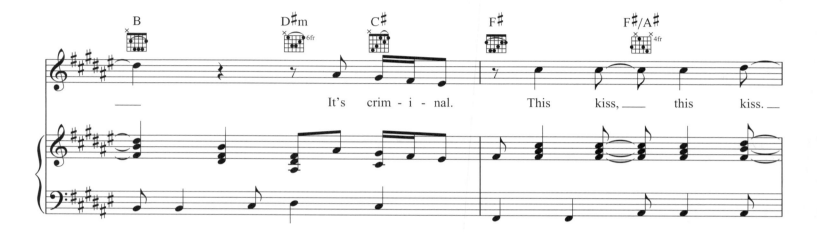

___ It's crim - i - nal. This kiss, ___ this kiss. ___

___ It's the way you love me, ba - by. ___

Repeat and Fade | **Optional Ending**

It's the way you love me, dar - ling. ___

THE THUNDER ROLLS

Words and Music by PAT ALGER
and GARTH BROOKS

Additional Lyrics

2. Every light is burnin' in a house across town.
   She's pacin' by the telephone in her faded flannel gown,
   Askin' for a miracle, hopin' she's not right,
   Prayin' it's the weather that has kept him out all night.
   And the thunder rolls, and the thunder rolls.
   Chorus

3. She's waitin' by the window when he pulls into the drive.
   She rushes out to hold him, thankful he's alive.
   But on the wind and rain, a strange new perfume blows,
   And the lightnin' flashes in her eyes, and he knows that she knows.
   And the thunder rolls, and the thunder rolls.
   Chorus

THREE WOODEN CROSSES

Words and Music by KIM WILLIAMS
and DOUG JOHNSON

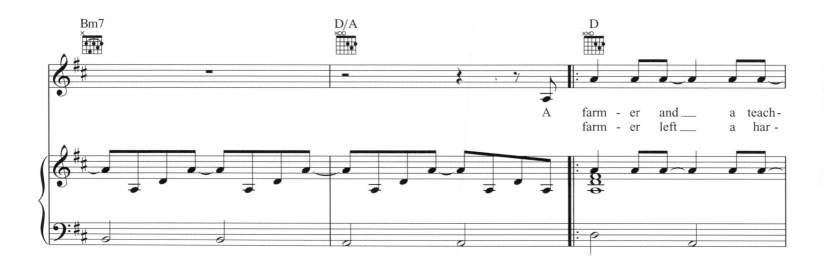

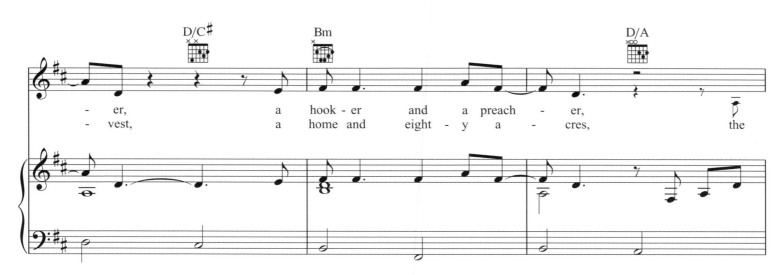

* Recorded a half step lower.

WHAT ABOUT NOW

Words and Music by RON HARBIN,
ANTHONY SMITH and AARON BARKER

Moderately fast

The sign __ __ in the win-dow said for sale or trade __ on the last __ re-main-ing din-o-saur

WHAT WAS I THINKIN'

Words and Music by BRETT BEAVERS,
DERIC RUTTAN and DIERKS BENTLEY

Beck-

By the think - in'

WHAT HURTS THE MOST

Words and Music by STEVE ROBSON
and JEFFREY STEELE

It's hard to deal __ with the pain of los - in' you ev - 'ry - where I go, __

I can take the rain __ on the roof of this emp - ty house, __

WHERE WERE YOU
(When the World Stopped Turning)

Words and Music by
ALAN JACKSON

Where were you when the world___ stopped turn-in' that Sep - tem - ber day?

Out in the yard___ with your wife and chil - dren or
Teach - in' a class___ full of in - no - cent chil - dren or

some kind __ of an-swer and look at your-self __ and what real-ly mat - ters?
mov - ie _____ you're watch-in' and

I'm just a sing-er of __ sim-ple songs. I'm not a

real po-lit-i-cal __ man. I watch C-N-N, __ but I'm not __

__ sure I can tell you the dif-f'rence in I-raq and I-ran. But

YOUR MAN

Words and Music by CHRIS DUBOIS,
CHRIS STAPLETON and JACE EVERETT

* Recorded a half step lower.

I can't be-lieve how much it turns___ me on___ just to be your man.___

WIDE OPEN SPACES

Words and Music by
SUSAN GIBSON

Who does-n't know what I'm talk-ing a-bout? __

315